Surgeonfish

for Gary + Judy McCann,
in friendship,
Ingrid

Surgeonfish

Poems by Ingrid Wendt

WordTech Editions

Published by WordTech Editions
P.O. Box 541106
Cincinnati, OH 45254-1106

Typeset in Aldine by WordTech Communications LLC, Cincinnati, OH

ISBN: 193345606X
LCCN: 2005932969

Poetry Editor: Kevin Walzer
Business Editor: Lori Jareo

Visit us on the web at www.wordtechweb.com

Cover: Painting by Nils-Aslak Valkeapää, "Uten tittel," 1991.

Acknowledgments

Grateful acknowledgment is made to the editors and publishers of the following magazines and anthologies in which some of these poems first appeared, a few in slightly different form and/or with different titles.

Anthropology and Humanism, "*Prego*"
Antioch Review, "Italy: Singing the Map"
Beloit Poetry Journal, "The History of Strife"
Calapooya Collage, "Pilgrim," "Lines Begun While Hearing Charles Wright
        Read," "Still Life," "Double *Rondeau* in December," "Museums"
Calapooya, "Road Kills"
Calliope, "Porcupine at Dusk"
Chariton Review, "Scaffolding," "First Morning in the Santa Caterina: Villa
        Serbelloni, Bellagio," "St. Martin's Day, *Lago di Como*," "10:30
        Sunday Morning"
Electric Rexroth, "Good Friday: Wendell, Idaho"
Ellipsis, "Canon"
Firefly Magazine, "Report from Tromsø"
Fireweed, "On the Nature of Family Travel"
GSU Review, "Mukilteo Ferry"
Many Mountains Moving, "Even the Stones Have Names," "Questions of
        Grace," "Words of Our Time"
Ms., "Taps"
Nimrod, "Finnmark, an Idyl"
Overtures, "Happy Days"
Petroglyph, "Poem in August"
Southern Poetry Review, "Sheep Creek Bay: Flaming Gorge, Utah"
The Texas Observer, "Surgeonfish" and "On the Use of Irony"
Weber Studies, "Special Effects," "Columbus and Me," and "Gas. 1940"
Wilderness, "The Thing to Do"

"Blessed Among Birds" first appeared in *The Sacred Place*, an anthology edited by W. Scott Olsen and Scott Cairns (Salt Lake City: University of Utah Press, 1996).

"Landing" first appeared in *Viewer's Guide to "William Stafford—the Life of the Poem."* Video by Michael Markee and Vincent Wixon. Ashland, Oregon: TTTD Productions.

"Monika, Before Reunification" first appeared in *Writing the World: On Globalization,* an anthology edited by David Rothenberg and Wandee J. Pryor. Cambridge, Massachusetts: MIT Press, 2005.

Grateful acknowledgment is made to the late Czeslaw Milosz for permission to reprint lines from his poem "One More Day," in *Unattainable Earth*.

The author wishes to thank the University of New Mexico for a fellowship at the D.H. Lawrence Ranch; the Rockefeller Study and Conference Center, Bellagio; and the Mary Anderson Center for the Arts, for periods of residence during which many of these poems were begun.

My thanks to Charles Wright for permission to publish the poem with his name in its title.

My thanks also to DAT, a Sámi publishing house and record company in Guovdageaidnu, Norway, for permission to use, as the cover of this book, the painting from Nils-Aslak Valkeapää's astonishing book of poems, paintings, and photographs: *Nu guhkkin dat mii lahka / Så fjernt det nære*, published in 1994. Learn more about DAT, their books, and Sámi music, at http://www.dat.net/main.html.

"Mukilteo Ferry" received the following honors in national contests: 3rd place, GSU national contest, 2003; Finalist, Jane Kenyon Award, 2003; Finalist, Iowa Review Award, 2003.

Many friends, trusted readers all, saw some of these poems in earlier (and sometimes finished) versions. Among them, for their insights and encouragement, I thank Jim Barnes, Martin Christadler, Tom Ferté, Helen Frost, Jerry Gatchell, Martha Gatchell, Mechthild Hesse, Marilyn Krysl, Eric Muller, Naomi Shihab Nye, H. Palmer Hall, Dell Hymes, Virginia Hymes, Myrna Peña-Reyes, David St. John, Bill Sweet, Judy Volem, Margot Volem, Patty Wixon, and Vince Wixon. Grateful thanks, also, to linguist Charles Ferguson, with whom I shared several enlightening conversations on the derivations of certain Italian words and their connections to our English tongue, as well as on the lives, histories, and symbologies of various Catholic saints.

Abiding love, admiration, and appreciation for my husband of thirty-six years, poet and writer Ralph Salisbury: companion in these many explorations (with often the patience of a saint, himself), from whom I continue to learn so much.

On the banks of the Tana, the Green, the Rio Grande
the Donner and Blitzen, Columbia, Rhine, Main
and the Snake

On the shores of Lake Como, of Sheep Creek Bay,
the Gulf of Aqaba,
Gulf of Suez, and Puget Sound

In front of the Pacific, in front of the Atlantic
the North, the Barents
and the Carribean Seas

On the altars of all hearts searching for truth, peace, and justice
including your own, dear reader,
I lay these words.

This book is dedicated to the memory of
Nils-Aslak Valkeapää (1943-2001)
renowned Sámi (Laplander) poet, painter, musician, and photographer
performer, opener of the 1994 Winter Olympics
and tireless recorder of the history, legends and stories
of his people in the North.
It is his painting ("Uten tittel," 1991)
on the cover.

And though the good is weak, beauty is very strong
Nonbeing sprawls, everywhere it turns into ash whole expanses of being,
It masquerades in shapes and colors that imitate existence
and no one would know it, if they did not know that it was ugly.

And when people cease to believe that there is good and evil
Only beauty will call to them and save them
So that they still know how to say: this is true and that is false.

—Czeslaw Milosz

Contents

Offerings

When they passed the collection plate and I asked
Where does the money go? my mother, ever
certain, whispered, *To God, for His work.*
Those words were enough

though for years
what use God had of money, I couldn't guess.
And when a young friend died?
God wanted her, too.

Those days, all of us knew there was no
question too great, nothing the right word
couldn't stop. *Why?* led straight
where we wanted to go. *If only* never

kept doubling back on
itself, and *courage*
was always a day we could step into
from the right side of the bed.

Now, when I learn of your grief
I look for those words that make everything right.
These words, my whole heart is in them.
This whisper, I pass it to you.

One

The Thing to Do

Though what I did that day was right,
reporting the rattlesnakes coiled tightly
together—diamond-backed lovers
blind to my step within a breath of
leaves crackling under the bush;

Though he did what he had to,
hacking them dead with his long-handled
garden hoe, flinging the still-
convulsing whips of their passion into
the bed of his pickup—that scene,

bright vulture of memory, stays;
picks this conscience that won't
come clean: this wasn't
the way the story would go
those times I wondered if ever

I'd see my own rattlesnake out in the wild,
having listened through years of summer
hikes, in the likeliest places, without
once hearing that glittering warning
said to be unmistakable; knowing

since childhood, the thing to do is not
flicker a muscle, to stare the face of danger
down as though it didn't exist.
No rattlesnake ever had eyes for another.
And menace never multiplied, one season to next.

Blessed Among Birds

Blessed among birds, is how my husband
likes to put it, and maybe it's true: that flock of
six or eight kinglets too young for their ruby red crowns or even

those characteristic white eye rings, flicking through our backyard
apple-tree leaves around my head so close I could have reached out and
touched each one as it clung upside down to a leaf, picking the

undersides clean, or perched on a twig—tip of beak to
tip of tail the length of my own little finger—fearlessly
sizing up my mountainous form frozen, like lava,

mid-motion, but
shining (surely the feeling
was shining) like gold,

the true Midas touch of their chip
chip-chipping
pitched so high the human ear almost

can't take it in. I know
my husband hasn't
Saint Francis in mind, although

when he says what he says about blessings, suddenly
here I am, as Giotto never painted me, high on the east
cathedral wall in Assisi, the upper

cathedral, built on top of that other, more somber
nave and transepts we studied so long (craning our necks to find
Biblical scenes preserved in all their brilliance by almost-

darkness) we almost
didn't have time for the brightness above: blue and gold
and light streaming through space so

unexpected our souls
were flying, the birds
hovering over the head of Saint Francis,

perched on his shoulder,
hadn't a thing
over us. No,

what he's remembering, when I mention the kinglets, is how
two weeks ago over in Eastern Oregon,
walking together near Benson Pond at dusk, I was

whacked on the head by a great horned owl.
I know this sounds
funny, and that

was my reaction, too: I laughed
although the whole top of my scalp throbbed
from the force of the blow. It was hard.

It felt like someone had taken a board flat
to the top of me, someone had sneaked
up from behind in that mystical field of knee-high grass

we waded through in half
light, finding the path to the cottonwoods faint
but true, and all of that empty sky ours.

But no one had told us this was a hard hat area, who
would have imagined *Danger*, lured by the hoot, hoot, soft
lullaby deep in the trees? *Athena,*

my husband said later, hoping to comfort,
Athena has tapped you, marked you with wisdom.
But wisdom was not what I felt, hunched into my collar, my eyes

following giant wings to their perch in the branches ahead.
And blessings were not right then first in my mind (although
later I saw again those claws that were blessedly not

extended), gaining my
balance,
discovering just

off to our right in the crook of a tree the owlet
so fluffy grey and rounded we thought at first it must
be a raccoon without a mask.

All of us caught
off guard. Unmoving,
all of us stunned into place.

Columbus and Me

Coming fresh to this Oregon soil the greatest thing
was to hike far from any human demand and to sit
looking over land empty of human influence far
as the eye could see—Horse Lake
catching the first rays of sun brushing between the Three
Sisters, ridge after rolling green
ridge misted in silence—or to camp
at a bend in some river large and level enough
for a tent, the simpler, we said, the better, our red
nylon parachute roped under some branch overhead and staked,
giant columbine, wide to the ground.
Twenty-four, and an ocean away from my Illinois home,

more than twenty years away from tonight—learning at last
the names *Kalapuya, Chinook, Takelma*, rethinking counties
Clackamas, Tillamook, Clatsop, Wallowa—how easy it was to sail,
certain as morning, into a landscape no one
human could ever have witnessed before.
Not this rock, that riffle.
Not this bird song leading us on, such bounty
falling into our hands.

Porcupine at Dusk

Out of the bunch grass
      out of the cheat grass
      a bunch of grass waddles
         my way.

Quill-tips bleached by winter four
      inches down: crown of glory dark
      at the roots: a halo
         catching the sun's
         final song:

No way could such steady
      oblivion possibly live
      up to legend, whatever
         fear I might have had
         is gone, but still I stop

Short on my after-dinner walk, no
      collision course if I
      can help it, thinking
         at first it's the wind,
         nudging a path out of the field

Or one of a covey of tumbleweed
      lost like those today on the freeway,
      racing ahead of my car that whole long drive
      here to the banks of the Snake, to friends
         so close they know
         when to leave me alone.

As though I were nowhere around, the porcupine
        shuffles the edge of the road,
        in five minutes crosses
                a distance I could have covered
                in less than one

And disappears at last into cattails
        and rushes, sunset, a vespers
        of waterbirds, leaving me
                still unwilling to move.

I am a sucker for scenes like this.
        The slowest beauty can rush me.
        And here I am,
                all of my defenses down.

Poem in August

1.
Where have they gone—that blue rush of
penstemons holding the line by the fence,

lupine holding the meadow
down. Towhees in

thickets. My ears
all summer ripe with song.

New here, myself, I
thought they lived here.

Just passing through, I said
this is where I belong.

2.
Higher up still
I know there's a meadow where all
over again it's June:

larkspur, penstemon, lupine begin
like a song held
back so long, when it's over

it's over too soon.
September without
summer.

Up higher, no calendar.
Blue
sky, breathless

blossoms: ice crystals out from the center
all year long
splitting stone.

3.
Yellow, come forward! Orange! Red!
Blue has slipped back into sky.

Were I such bold colors I'd be impatient.
Blue, begone! But you

have waited your turn for larkspur, penstemon,
heads bowed between fingers of lupine: here

is the church, here is the steeple —
flashy your rabbitbrush feathers,

foolscap firecrackers,
peaks on stalks rising

higher each day, small
suns of mallow cupped simple

as dawn, the perfect
Easter bonnets resurrected so late

not even autumn will find you, the right
colors already, taking your own sweet time.

Lawrence Ranch, Taos, New Mexico

Canon

Close as a secret
Jones Hole Fish Hatchery keeps between
itself and shores of Green River,

there's a canyon tucked under a sky so high only one
red wall at a time sees sun.

Last week, five hours the only human around,
I followed that course: Jones Creek eternally
baptizing watercress; cottonwoods' gold

confessing my feet; my soul expanding,
expanding, no words

could have contained it.
No echoing nave.
No dome.

The trail register asked for remarks.
"Beautiful," "Great," "Stupendous," some said.

"Better than Zion, without the crowds."
It was time to go home. Yet one
caught the last of the sun:

"All this earth, and
I, a creature on it."

Benediction ringing
each step back to the car.
Company, all that long drive back to town.

Epithalamion from Norway

Eden, Eden, but who
would have dreamed Genesis

here in the Arctic: *Nordkap*
that tourist obsession Ralph and I last month succumbed to

for hours our little red rental car bearing us north, north, north,
noon

at our backs: heaven,
sea, darkness, light, rocks—smooth

moons marking the spot the land simply stops
insisting: timberline sinking

right into the sea
or is it emerging? Friends,

how long have we thought of the Garden
as jungle? as warm?

Friends, I have dived in these waters:
cobalt blue of *fjord* and a silent chorus of *sei* iridescent

around me, patient
angels, watchful. Here

the future begins.
Here, I have walked on waves of tundra

golden with autumn lichen and mosses and every
shade of red and orange from sunrise to sunset and

here the future
begins. Nightly,

into the frozen sky, green
wings of flame—and white—and blue—spiral

from the horizon, sway
over my head

and again, it's Eden, it's heaven, over
and over the world begins.

It is love. Yours.
These words, today.

Your own.

Finnmark, an Idyl

At the poet's house, remote
among the absent swallows
(empty, their nests under
the eaves), the poet's windows
are open, and a different bird
sings from a heart that could be

my own, in the sun (that soon
for two winter months will be gone)
now blessing our shoulders, our feet,
my skin, fresh from the sauna,
tingling, this golden expansion
new friendship brings; and I

for a while can pretend I don't
hear the poet tell about the five
or six kinds of birds this year
that never, like me, have
been here before, this far
to the north, which has never

in memory been so warm. It's said
they now can survive here. It's said
there are too many homes in the landscape
they come from. Bird, for a while
I truly was glad to see you.
Bird, I took joy in your song.

This Side of Paradise

Sunrise, and soon above the pound and rumble and right at the edge
of the surf, the first

two-man beach patrol of the day will once again hunt the invisible
(no one, no one, walks the beach in that direction) and soon

this Black-Crowned Night Heron
once again will be gone.

Every day near sunset this heron has come. And gone
wherever herons go after sundown. And returned again the next
      morning.

And always it's planted itself at the edge of the same shallow pool: mild
gargoyle poised forever over its own stubby reflection, what fish

Could be frightened by this? Or do fish look up? And could the Snowy Egret
high-stepping through densely green treetops guess we watch with binoculars?

(Look at those branches sway. Those spindly legs: the way they
pull the air like invisible chewing gum, slow motion.) Dance so implausible,

awkward, the mere fact this bird can balance at all, had us newcomers calling it
Fearless, after the tv special on Darwin's less famous discovery:

island creatures evolving with no natural predators:
humans once could come as close as skin.

Fearless ourselves, the first few days, the way we didn't know these
dune buggy drivers, cruising the water's edge: how they were really police.

And then we saw that word in all capitals: black
letters filling up the fronts and backs of their bright yellow t-shirts,

their everyday presence filling the twenty feet or less between our own
iron-barred and tightly-screened porch, and half the palm-fringed
        world beyond:

that once-postcard-perfect aquamarine: filmy,
cataract-gray.

Sheep Creek Bay: Flaming Gorge, Utah

Sunset above, and sunset reflecting
pink and orange on already
brick-red bluffs, leaden
water, and nothing

in sight alive. What was I expecting?
A regular lake, I think, with berries
along the bank, and rushes; some mention
of green, some comfort

after a long day's drive connecting
points on a map, hunters all day prowling the highway
shoulders, waving me on. I've been
where the earth once

broke its back and never mended—
rib after downward slanting rib forever
committed to sky. I've been in
the canyon below where last year some

family wasn't able to run for it, never suspecting
that one simple creek could overnight plunder
all of their beds, along with its own.
And what do we make of this? Down

below me, the world's largest collection
of tire tracks: so many fixed grins of summer
from hundreds of boat trailers, camper vans. And
the rest of my plan: to travel on

(if I can beat the sun) to dinosaur footprints etched
along a lake years before earth's most colossal blunder
ever; according to printed guides, best seen
in the shadows of sunset or dawn.

Who has the heart for this? Who needs more evidence?
Who will believe it means something to find just one
set of rabbit tracks. Fresh. And fresher than scent,
the single-minded trail of coyote loping along.

Road Kills

The first time it happened my boyfriend (not
really my boyfriend, but someone to take the place of one
who'd just dumped me) was driving. *Splat:* right
into the windshield a dove (a dove!) and
right on beat it ricocheted off before our hearts
could take in their wound. Tom didn't slow down, of course,

just as there was no question of stopping—*that* course
I've learned from poems and family cautions is open not
to little guys, nor is swerving allowed. Your heart's
in your throat, it's on the brake you want to slam but damn, someone
might be behind you, the road might be slick, and so on, and
so, So long, rabbit, snake, toad, I've got the right

of way; grown up, I've learned to lose count. Kate's right,
too, not mourning the deer she couldn't avoid. In the course
of two days I hear her tell the story at least four times and
each time the same conclusion, the same surprise: It's not
so hard to be philosophical! Grown up, it's something one
does, one hardens what's left of the left-out heart.

So much for success. New question: How long do hearts
keep quiet like this, or do they just give up their right-
ful place in the mouth? Words, words, there's a new one
for every occasion. Last week on TV, a Bill Moyers course
in survival, neighborhood violence, little girls saying *It's not
so bad, all of us gots to die sometime, my time is coming*, and

I know somewhere out there's a bullet, with my name on it—when
will convention break down? Will we notice? Take it to heart?

What to say to the stranger I met walking the dog: it's not
his fault our country's such a mess, and *Hey, it ain't right*
he says, *But if this government's ever going to get back on course*
there has to be bloodshed, we have to go back to square one.

And this is the country where almost every single one
of my own friends and relatives every day and
night for nearly a year stayed tuned in to the course
of a murder trial the media let us all partake in. Eat your heart
out, Perry Mason, this was the Real Thing, live, in color, right
out of the best Clue game ever invented, were we playing or not?

But we were overseas. Out of it. Hard, returning, to put our hearts
where our mouths were, trying to fit back in. We managed. But
        wasn't that right?
Could any verdict possibly go against stardom? (Dared we ask?)
        Of course not.

Two

Questions of Grace

1.
Somehow, it's cows we've decided are stupid.
And pigs. Chickens, too, therefore all the more
edible, though we deplore the conditions they
sometimes are raised in, egg to hatchet

cramped on the assembly line, never scratching
gravel as they were born to do, or cocking a voice
to the sun. Some of my friends, of course, will eat
only that which is brainless, which never had

even the slightest song of its own. To whom
but the Norwegians can I confess not only have
I eaten reindeer stew, salami, blood balls, but
last night, here in Norway, I ate Vågehval, Lesser

Rorqual, *Balaenoptera Acutorostrata*, yes, last night
I ate a steak of whale, tender and
thick as filet mignon. It was good.

2.
Ánde Somby, Sámi lawyer, son
of reindeer herders descended from
reindeer herders farther back than anyone
knows, tells how when his father had to kill
one of his own he talked to it, petted it, "Deer,
I'm sorry you happened to be here just at this
wrong time. Whose fault is it I do this?"

Here in Sámiland, all is used. I've seen
the way the skin of the skull is stretched
on birch-twig frames just the right size for boots;
and sinew turns into thread; antlers, to buckles;
bones, to straws to filter drinking water.
I think of the Coos, the Takelma, the Kalapuya back home.

All but the Coos are gone.

3.
Last week at the Tromsø museum, I learned two
or three coastal villages still are allowed to
hunt for whale, and in each village, five
to ten boats, and in each boat, a five

to ten-whale limit, May through July, adults
only; and always some government person's on board,
testing the meat, researching, counting. Twenty
thousand left in these waters, no fear

of extinction. I learned the whalers, following still
the steps of their parents, their parents' parents before them
(once feeding not only their children but also the life
blood of Norway) would certainly profit more today, fishing cod.

4.
Years, now, and my mother
each time we visit, wrestles
the question of grace.

> *God is great, God is good,*
> *and we thank Him for our food.*

That's ok, she says, but

> *By His goodness we are fed,*
> *give us, Lord, our daily bread,*

why ask for what we've already got?

You're right, we tell her.
We say the grace again.
We eat.

5.
Back home, our neighbors, the few
Sundays we ate with them, they
made up something new each time.

We heard the grievous errors of our ways.
We heard again the sin of our ingratitude.
We heard the names of all those needing blessing,

including ourselves. Heavenly Father, the food
always got cold.

6.
Late afternoon and the Tromsø sky again
has drifted shut, a solid white porcelain bowl, hill
to hill, except for one small overlay, one
single stretch of silver, long as a squid, the shiny lure

Siri (eleven) cast again and again last week in the Tana River,
Harald rowing against the current almost an hour

to keep us in place, the reeds along the bank
promising *strike*, the pools where grayling for decades

used to hide and in past years have disappeared and then
the reeling it in, such happiness, six inches long,
the skinny dumb fish she picked up and kissed and kissed and
later, for supper, ate.

7.
And still, I've found a restaurant here in town with
dishes I can't bring myself to eat: bear bouillon
(with rye bread and butter); barbequed bear ribs; grilled
bear fillet; Siberian bear meat casserole. Is it
just personal?

                         For the Sámi, the bear is a sacred
animal; hunting it, eating it, everyone knows the rules.
What would they think if they knew that I myself once
talked with a bear in the wilds, persuaded that bear
to leave me alone?

And what if I'd talked with a whale?

8.
By what sign in the market
do we know the spirit?

By what rituals
are we permitted to eat it?

9.
Reader, somewhere in the coast range
of Oregon, have you heard about this? some
physicist somehow wired a grove of trees for sound.

When one
tree was cut down, it emitted a cry.
When that tree cried, the rest of the grove cried, too.

10.
Green things: spinach, peas, cabbage, kale,
zucchini, pole beans, broccoli, dill, how to
measure the songs of that chorus of chlorophyll?

11.
And who is to say the rocks are not
also alive? And the hills?
Last week I walked over tundra.
What from the car seemed barren, forlorn,
was totally covered with mosses, lichen, every
color of sunset, horizon
to horizon.
                          And at the coast, at home,
trying to gather mussels, go fishing,
the stones we clamber over, what barnacles just
starting out do we crush? What larvae
of starfish, silent as galaxies, just
that far from our own recognition?

Last week a poet showed me a stone,
the size of a football, smoother than skin.
Hold it, he said, with care.
Between your hands, it will breathe.

12.
Reader, what
day do we not trade
at least one voice for our own?

Where,
and with what words
do we dare place our feet?

Three

Lines Begun While Hearing
Charles Wright Read

Again this word *nothing*, so much lament.
Why do I feel such joy?

Naming things: some say the act takes them away.
Mysterious bird skipping golden and black through branches:
sunlight and shadow. Call it *Goldfinch*, it's gone.

All these places I too have been but left
unwritten: never lost, that new person
there I could have become.

Far from home, so much becomes possible!
Sirens of Greece. The Rhine's Lorelei.

Tonight, the loss of nothing but fear.

Tromsø. Frankfurt. Bellagio.
All the poems I never had thought to write
singing my name.

On the Nature of Family Travel

Three months of more togetherness
Than we had bargained for: often
Just one small hotel room, all three of us
Each night trying to find the right
Cheap restaurant, ways to pass
Evening hours with even our playing cards wearing
Thin; how we rejoiced, at last

For one whole month, a house of our own!
Privacy! Not that it hadn't been good. Daily each
Museum had opened us up, each castle truly fulfilled
The promise of guidebooks. Yet who could not
Bless this new freedom, even walking each day
To market? Cooking again! Where we were
Privilege rang, and every morning we answered,

Never knowing just what we'd hear.
One day we drove to the moors. They were near
And said to be where you could get lost.
We parked at the first steep rise, climbed
Stile and floundering hill (wave
Or dune, who could tell which?), waded
Heather that really was purple, clouds

Below us and clouds above, aiming for
One of the ridges billowing over us, dipping down,
Climbing; green ridges around us everywhere
Singed with sky, startled with sheep; and we,
Together with the clouds scurrying, hurrying
Back to each other, calling out *Look!*
Come farther! Come here!

Report from Tromsø

Friends, here at the end of August, lilacs—two
storeys tall—have just finished blooming, and strawberries
start to arrive from the North. Mushrooms
(the kind we pick at home in November) are popping
up in woods all over the crest of this island we live on, quite
cosmopolitan, really, except for the magpies (Eastern

Oregon, here on the fjord!) and seagulls squabbling
past our 5th-floor window no matter what hour,
my earplugs get plenty of use, and the whole
world revolves around fish. (Surprise, Galileo!)
(Or was it Copernicus? Who paid attention?
Nothing that central could ever again change direction.)

Last night, quite unlike ourselves, we were out
on the town till dawn. 1: 30. Instead of on the eastern
horizon, Cassiopeia showed up right up over our heads,
the first stars we've seen, can you believe, since June.
The moon was too far South, where it doesn't belong.
And when the sun for weeks wouldn't go down,

when that end-of-the-day everyone banks on
to let the body retreat, the mind to suspend, never
would come, we found we really could against all odds
maintain equilibrium: coasting on light, becoming light:
off and on all day on some kind of cruise control.
Could we be angels? Heretical. Maybe. But here

when clock says morning, the sun's in the North!
And the map is all wrong: North Pole, in the center,

completely encircled by upside-down Canada,
Finland, Greenland, Russia: all we ever called home
off in the left-hand corner. Not only our heads
turning around but

every last thing we never
suspected was holding us down.
How important it's been, being right at that Center.
Goodbye, dear anchors! Someone says
Let's go fishing, at midnight? We pay
attention. Believe me. We go.

Still Life

Britt, had I been driving, I wouldn't have
stopped the car where you did. Right then my own
focus was far over the rise: finally surfacing, this
top right edge of northeastern Norway, higher up even than

Vardø (that dot on the map, that scar
retreating Germans once burned onto the thumb
of the left hand of Finnmark): this
rocky shoreline flat

up against the Barents Sea, magnified
beyond imagining, here where the world's largest
bulldozer finally came to the end of the line, how
could my camera possibly capture the size of that rubble: Titanic

after Titanic slabs frozen all
the way to the northern horizon in that
impossible angle all history books show.
But this is where you stopped the car,

and with the children, clattered down the steep
slope of the shoulder, bent over a cluster of rust-
colored stones: rounded, smooth, small
fists a river could have left behind (except

this was the side of a mountain), their surfaces blossoming ice-
green, almost chartreuse, and yellow and orange; white; black;
scab-like; infinitesimal spore-prints of distant galaxies;
sea spume, petrified: this unexpectedly beautiful

lichen, surviving eons of Arctic winter (and now,
all those miles in the trunk, on the plane), and blooming, still,
in this still life of stones gathered together on my
coffee table like lilac petals, geraniums—flowers within

flowers—because you said I should take them back to Tromsø,
thousands of miles from home, where I never expected some days
to feel myself adrift and close to sinking under too
many impressions, the whole wide world

off-center. This sun,
where I never have seen it before.
Those truant stars, my sense of direction.
Myself, at the end of the birds' own migration.

How to make sense of it all?
This borrowed apartment five stories over the ground.
Picking me up, each time I look back at that image of you,
looking down. Before me, these treasured, hospitable stones.

Even the Stones Have Names

Here is where we live, I'm pointing (Harald
translating). Mountains, here where it's green,
east and west of our city, no more than an hour's
drive to go skiing, or to the beach, and Eugene
has just about everything: opera, ballet, health
foods, tofu (all week I've been planning this scene),

and here is Tucson. My mother lives in Tucson.
Here in Arizona. (I've brought the map with me,
pictured this route to sharing our lives, in Finnmark;
something to offer Harald's mother, Kristine.)
Three days by car, to Tucson, it's that far away.
But she was born in Michigan. That's even

farther. My sister's in upstate New York.
And here is Illinois, the place I'd dream of,
if I dreamed of home. I grew up in town,
and Ralph, on an Iowa farm his sister's keeping
going. Our daughter's in Italy, working.
She's fine. We try not to worry. This scene,

just as I envisioned, back home in Eugene.
But something else has been added—our week with Harald
and Britt, with Kristine—and without warning, between us,
invisible, swaggering, there for all of us
to see, that old assumption: it's natural, leaving
behind our family, our home. Yesterday Harald took us

past the birches he used to get lost in—between
his mother's house, where he was born, and the house

his father's brother built (now his own)—green
leaves deeper than green, full of midnight
sun, and a tangle of flowers I'd never dreamed
survived here—took us down to the river to fish.

Past the place the German army, retreating,
burned the turf hut where his mother was born.
Past the salmon nets—all those centuries leaning
into the current, rows of wooden poles
bedded in Sámi tradition—and past the creeks
whose mouths on the Tana have always offered fish

whose names Harald told us, and told us, *Here
in Tana, even the stones have names*. Yesterday,
the sun on our backs, with Harald and Aslak and Siri,
the sun off-center, each moment was full of forever.
This map was a way I thought we'd meet each other.

This map is a stone in my heart.

Pilgrim

Gypsy, my father once told me, *it's part of our name.*
Wendt from *Wendland*, from *land of wanderers*. Still,
my favorite romance was that this heritage came
from my Austrian grandmother. Born on the boat to Chile,
Francesca Weisser—who died, before I was born,
about the time my runaway father was rounding Cape Horn

bound for Germany—rumor was, she had gypsy
blood, too. So when I phone my mother
from Norway, and once again she wistfully
prods, *have you gotten this out of your system?*, what
can I say? My friend Helen tells me she once
tugged a canoe free from river-bank mud

and the next day a memory surfaced through muscle,
through more than forty years: herself as a child
struggling a turtle, dead, from leaves and mud till
her hands held wonder: *maybe what's happened is filed*
within us, our bodies remember what minds cannot.
How else to describe it? And how to explain it's not

just adventure I'm after, but what the inner
world has in store: reflections of earth's geography
buried so deep in the system, each country I visit,
each new landscape tugs, tugs, and the country
within the body responds. Lungs, in Eastern
Oregon, opening, lungs unfurling, they'd turn

the body inside out, if they could, greeting
the sky, informing me, *this is where you belong.*
And look at Italy, all of the senses meeting
as one: resurrected, the skin drinking song,
and color, and light baptizing the tongue,
saying *this, this is your home.* No longer young,

and still, no end to this road. The way in Chile
the heart, overfull, finds hearts to contain it. The voice
in Germany, tuned with its own. And now in Norway
the feet, for the first time ever, knowing the source
of their song: earth's anchor—gentle, that shudder
of glacier, mountain, fjord—solid under

bones connecting to bones, what holds us together
resonant, what the body always has known.
Roald Amundsen, what did you tell your mother?
Did your blood, the closer you came to the pole,
get dizzy with gravity? Did you let yourself hear
in your ecstatic pulse, a mother's moan? Her fear?

Prego

Ask for something, *Per*
favore, please, the answer is
Prego. Please.

Thank you, *Grazie*, thank you,
you say. Instead of you're welcome?
Prego. The answer is please.

Prego, listen, here in Italy, every
time you think you're polite, this lift
of the verbal eyebrow, this rise

and fall of the voice like a hand
on its way to your shoulder, insistent
lifeline picking you up,

letting you go
again. No problem! *Prego*
pulls up the covers and tucks you in.

Cape of Saint Martin. Communion
wafer on each Italian tongue. *Prego*.
Please, *Prego*, I pray to you,

Prego, don't
worry. Let me
do something for you.

Scaffolding

Bill, I call. *Elena*. *Help*. This printer won't print, my characters
somehow, it tells me, are wrong, the machine here won't take them,
and this, after all that last-minute scouting in Frankfurt, finally finding

in the red light district the proper transformer to let my own little
Japanese-made, American laptop plug into your updated sixteenth-century
wall here in Bellagio, Italy, where on the other side of these

immaculate floor-to-ceiling white curtains in this room that for two
blessed weeks I'm calling my own, another team all morning has been erecting
scaffolding: pipe by long, rusty pipe clanging

gradually upward over sheets of plastic protecting patio bricks, over
boards and the bursts of hammers, curses, laughter, whatever
lizards that once may have sunned themselves out in the open are gone.

Song of the *Petti Rosso*, silenced. Silent, until this morning, the songs of stones
crumbling: earth, atom by atom, shifting, settling down for future
centuries, decades, or just how long has it been since the last

repair job on that opposite wall holding back half of the hill: its small
concrete fountain a slight indentation, its steps from this ground-floor office
to gardens terraced row upon row, where we stroll among roses and

cypresses, loquats, magnolias, persimmon trees, palms
ringed with the fragrant gray *Phlomis*, with lavender; *Santolina*
and rosemary; ivy, wisteria, maidenhair ferns, *Quinquefolia*: wall

towering over the road, where *Pinus Jeffreyi* tower over
us and their roots plunge down and through stones and mortar,
holding together earth and time and the chance

for us to be here, to drive or walk up this hill on a road built on yet
other walls, the first time I thought it was earth below our feet, but no,
from down below you see the arches, you see the years of human

scaffolding: patience of rock and patience of workers
like those outside this window again today, to whom these words
I thought I had to right away print, are nothing compared to the boards

tomorrow their lives
will depend upon, these
words I keep on believing will hold something up.

First Morning in the Santa Caterina:
Villa Serbelloni

after a line by Naomi Shihab Nye

I come to this studio tired.
I come, grim pilgrim in search of solitude,
dragging computer and notebooks, projects and rough
drafts like so many sacks of potatoes and no appetite.

I come here this morning with no design or ritual, no
cockle shells, beans in my shoes; my nerve ends for five weeks
uprooted by sightseeing, slowly shutting down to experience,
how much luxury can the spirit survive?

Saint Catherine of Siena is said to have levitated.
A painting in the shrine of her birthplace shows her
floating up the stairs, her mother below her, wondering
what in the world's going on. My mother back home trusts

my feet will be on the ground, never imagining me in some square
tower bearing Saint Catherine's name, perched among birds
on a hillside over *Lago di Como*, more than two hundred years ago
the retreat for a monk whose name I never will know.

I come to this tower, its stucco exterior patched
many times over and gray as the once-bare stones of the hill
cropping up through imported soil now washing away; gray tower
with one faded marigold face and squat cowl of capuchin red tiles.

I come to this tower door, hand-hewn and beautiful in its simplicity.
Door sturdy as armour: row after row of iron nails joining inner to
outer planks darkened by years of dark weather and lacquer. Door
whose nails inside are all bent back, flat, to the wood.

And suddenly, light, light, through windows taller than I am.
Light on branches of holly, branches of pine. Light in between.
And suddenly, bird songs. And here I am, swept up
in something so big it must surely be ecstasy.

No other word for it. Everything
matters, terribly. This
solid, wooden desk curved into the corner.
Vaulted ceiling I have to crane my neck to see.

Leaf I pick up from the rough stones inside the door.
Leaf, with the single pine needle my shoe has tracked in, I lay
on this thin-lipped altar of windowsill. Three whole weeks
with no duty but each day to live worthy of beauty, beginning with now.

10:30 Sunday Morning

Above Bellagio and all the town bells
Break loose. Plump

Vowels, they clunk together
Like *bocce* balls,

Jostle this literate hill
With the text

Of their joyful dissonance:
Phonemes, morphemes,

Syllables grouping and trying again
In a different rhythm.

And over the lake the competition
Chiming in. Listen!

It's pigeon season. And when
The bells stop,

Pop! goes a shotgun. Again
And again. Not much

Salvation there. Nor in the message
Funneling out

And over the lake from Varenna,
The car in the tunnel

Gunning its motor; frankly secular,
Even vernacular,

Roars of scooters unsettling
Tourists below.

How much the world calls to us!
And in the wake

Of the seaplane scattering gulls:
Under waves,

The meditations of snails. On this hill,
Extant, the scripture

Of fallen leaves our feet for weeks
Have been learning by heart.

St. Martin's Day, *Lago di Como*

1.
Silk scarves in all the tourist shops of Bellagio and,
our first weekend in town, one old woman tells us
soon she'll close down, it's November, today

she's selling them cheap and if we want to
buy one later, her name will be on the door,
her number, she'll come

whenever we call, the shawl
will be waiting, and do we know
this is the time of Saint Martin, surely we've heard of

the soldier who split his cape in two, for the beggar?
This weather, these last days of sun, your Indian Summer,
she says, it covers us, keeps us a bit longer warm. Warming

us, these words
in threads of our own foreign tongue.

2.
So we, too, call it the time of Saint Martin:
blue light etching the air, each leaf on each olive tree
silver and shining: grass on the hillside full to

bursting with green, gold, and the lake flat up against
mountains: each atom of empty space tangible,
sharp as the bite into apples. And sun

every day blessing our shoulders, the last of the roses,
cosmos, ivy red against ancient stones where lizards
dart across silence and one leaf after the other tumbles

hand over hand, down this starting-to-crumble
retaining wall. Later, one puff of wind and beech leaves
go sailing: so many handfuls of gold

coins settling: wishes to hold days like these
in mind forever. Mantles against what's to come.

3.
Saint Martin, patron of armorers, beggars and calvary,
coopers, domestic animals, girdlers and glovers, horses and
horsemen, innkeepers and millers, tailors, wine-merchants,

wool-weavers, called on in cases of drunkenness, storms and ulcers,
who would have guessed your day is the same as our Veteran's Day,
once called Armistice Day -- not because you were the first

conscientious objector, that aspect for hundreds of years,
long gone. I think of that little, not-too-old chapel outside
Cadenabbia, below *Capella San Martino*, scenic over the lake.

Each side of the altar, lists of *caduti*. *Paroli, Alessandro.*
Paroli, Battista. Casartelli, Pietro. Casartelli, Stefano.
Ortelli: Domenico, Egidio, Mario. Ortelli, Innocente.

Brothers. Cousins. Fathers. Sons. And by
whose hand? The Russians? The Germans? Our own?

4.

Again and again I am struck by the goodness of strangers.
Shopkeepers, bus drivers, old women in black, offering
more than directions. Unacknowledged,

the courage of small civilities. Who among them has
someone to hold them even one minute a day?
In the secret linings of smiles, how many legends of loss?

And those who keep faith with memory. Chapel.
Capella. Cape. A verbal procession all the way back to
Saint Martin. How far one small gesture goes on.

White on this hill over Bellagio, ground covers of
Christmas Roses begin to bloom in November.
Someone has to have planted them. Someone not

with us to see them. Will we pass it along?
Have you seen the flowers? The forest is sprouting snow!

Italy: Singing the Map

Varenna, *Ravenna*, *Verona*: listen!
Each day the same call for vespers, the same
church bells—five, or six, or seven—shifting
places and rhythm, the way each name

(*Carerra*, *Ferrara*, *Volterra*) can be
rung like a chord—dominant, tonic,
subdominant—each village diocese
superimposed over the lake. Phonics

(*Bellamo*, *Milano*, *Lugano*) like beads
on a rosary; hallowed, the sounds the tongue
makes of experience, echoing. One needs
practice, though, and alertness. What

if Augustus (*Assisi*, *Brindisi*, *Frasassi*)
had tried to exchange *Ichia* for *Carpi*,
instead of *Capri*? What if you, trying
to get to *Merano*, its castle, started

out for *Murano*? You (*Cortona*, *Cremona*,
Crotone) would enjoy the museum of glass.
Perhaps it's the same as with fauna
and flora: that one subtle accent—

glossy or dull black cap (*Arezzo*,
Tremezzo, *Bomarzo*)—telling us Marsh Tit
or Willow Tit. Hidden, the presence
of gills distinguishing Amanita

from Puffball. It's serious business,
this verbal bouquet: each village, each town
(Geranium, Chrysanthemum, Delphinium)
proud of its own unique chromosomes.

Each village, each town, a place (*Laglio*)
that just might (*Menaggio*) try to elope
with your heart (*Aureggio*). Learn to
sing its name. Love it well (*Bellagio*).

Double *Rondeau* in December

Grounds keepers, raking, raking, all day, every day,
Five whole weeks we're here and even in rain they
Haven't let up. Leaves of larch and leaves of beech;
All over this hill a forest planted three centuries
Back to look accidental: fifty-two acres

Of soil hauled in to cover this mountain of rock, a place
Only the very rich can create, and maintain. We're taking
Our pleasure here, too, our privileged feet keeping at least three
                              full-time grounds keepers raking,

Each day in a different location:
Below the round studio, Japanese maple;
Black walnut and figs on the terrace; birch, sweet
Cherry and poplar, loquat, persimmon; ginkgo and kew near
Tennis courts no one plays on, but just in case,
                              kept clear by groundskeepers raking.

Grounds keepers, raking gravel, packed earth and sand; making
Seashell designs in the driveways, bare ribs of roots; replacing
Yesterday's footprints along with their own, how does it seem
To be speeding up history? Did Leonardo da Vinci really
Walk this hill? Before him, Pliny? What will be left of today?

My first days here I swore before leaving there'd be no trail
My feet would not know. Three main ways to the castle, the lake
A hundred meters below, and miles crisscrossing between, cleaned
                    by invisible grounds keepers, raking.

How could I have known my love for this place would blaze
With the white fire of diamonds. That I would be taking
Leave with a grief fiercer than I could have foreseen.
Five whole weeks this forest, these trails, have seemed
Our own. How easy it's been, forgetting our place.
                    And the grounds keepers, raking, raking.

Museums

It is sometimes too much, this dutiful trek through art.
Everything calls to us. All these rooms and each
One full of possible revelations, beauty
Beyond translation, but the feet say they hurt,
The eyes are tired of jumping back and forth between
Title and canvas, drinking in the usual

Saints and still lifes, the hundreds of hours poured
Into each one, so many, we skim them like cream.
All these spiritual calories, who can digest them?
Still, I remember times I've been suddenly floored
By color. Or motion, frozen. Whatever the reason,
Something has given me just a taste of delirium.

I remember my climb to the top of Multnomah Falls.
Fearless, the swoon of pigeons swirling and silver,
Silent under the rim. And hiking down, that final bend,
Unexpected, that roar, that long throat of water, God's
Laughter, filling me, nothing need ever come after.
Genesis. All that beginning again.

Landing

Beneath us, our own shadow, rising to meet us:
this bullet with wings, this missile
effortless over the clouds,

                            centered

bull's-eye in its own
perfectly rainbowed target
cruising as we cruise down to families, jobs,
certainty looming larger and larger to join us.

                                            Above us,
behind us, all that innocent blue: clear forever.
All that forever. And ever. And ever.

Four

Surgeonfish

What I don't tell Glen, when I respond to his prize-winning fourth-
grade novel about the Spined Avenger, could fill
another book

> *and has done, and keeps on*
> *being rewritten, rewritten*
> *although it really can be*

scary, I tell him, I know from experience, yes, that fish
really will attack, you've chosen your brave
protagonist well. But Ralph and I were swimming

too close, I tell him, to spawning grounds—eggs, or newly-hatched
young—or maybe that leveled-off part of the
reef was their own

> *last night on tv, the foreign*
> *minister saying: For some, it's always been Land*
> *that must be defended; for others, it's Life;*

and the surgeonfish,

two of them, named for the bright orange, scalpel-sharp
fins at the base of the tail, striking
from out of the blue, head on, then swerving:

> flak glancing the whole

length of our bodies, again and again. We must have looked funny,
flailing, thrashing the surface, like runners dodging a sniper,
like puppets unstrung.

But they were beautiful. That's
what we'd come for (such color!) the neon
indigo stripes of the black-scaled surgeonfish, neon

indigo edging the top and bottom black fins, edging the tail;
that pectoral fin, close to the gills: such a bright daffodil
sun! And this just one of so many others named in my book

and on Glen's video game. (They're real!) And here we swam
(I draw for him, his carpet our sand): the Gulf of Aqaba,
Gulf of Suez, around the tip of the Sinai

>   *behind us, that many-*
> *storied mountain, the sacred remains of Saint Catherine,*
> *somewhere the spot where Moses received God's Law*

we swam,

> *behind us, Magic Lake, not far inland: the whitest sand,*
> *the water a turquoise like nothing we'd ever seen, we posed*
> *for photos*

Glen, your resolution, I tell him, is wonderfully
balanced. Mature: the way the Spined Avenger saves
the reef from Scarface, the shark: without

fighting. They sign an agreement.

> *What is the whole, or even half of the story?*
> *Our guide, Mr. Jamal, in the last, the Six-Day War,*
> *fought at Magic Lake; where we posed, he saw men fall.*

I don't say Israel. Egypt. Anwar Sadat. Rabin.
Mr. Jamal, our guide, didn't use wet suit or fins.
The currents were strong. Only an arm away

to our left, the reef dropped off into darkness.
Down, down, two thousand feet down.
And all we could see was beauty.

November 1995

On the Use of Irony

1.
Wouldn't *you* laugh? The pickup ahead on
the road to school, its bumper sticker

I *DO* OWN THE ROAD

Both you and the owner knowing
better, that's part of being grown up
that's part of the fun, knowing

where this is coming from, shooting
down if not the original speakers at least
the challenge, with words of your own.

2.
And do we laugh, hearing the canned
laughter that goes with the sitcom set in *Natural Born
Killers,* knowing that when the father molests the daughter, we

Don't have to take it to heart? The director is playing,
like in *Pulp Fiction,* it's violence mocking itself: food
for wit, how smart to know it, let moralists say what they will.

3.
That eight year-old kid in the hallway, the big guy,
pushing the little one down.

He *does* own the road. He knows how to read.
He's seen that sticker, too, with his own eyes.

Happy Days

One night after "the Fonz"—who believe it or not
once played Scrooge in *A Christmas Carol*—*That's Incredible*
informed my daughter that hundreds of years ago Nostradamus

predicted the San Francisco earthquake and fire. World War One.
        Hiroshima. More. So
next morning, because I knew the value of books we looked in the library
        for data
also on vampires

(hunting the very same pictures a playmate
has shown her). Silent film heroines.
Princess stories

(forgotten, my failure the night she was three and I saw the first star,
taught "Make a wish" and she did,
"Mommy is there a crown on my head?").

Some other believer beating us to it. Finding out what to myself
I said (putting Nostradamus all the same on reserve) we had
all the time in the world to learn.

Special Effects

At Fort Ebey State Park, Washington

Finding the tunnel completely camouflaged into the whole
long side of the bluff, native grasses long ago

reclaiming empty cannon emplacements under a roof
so unnaturally flat it tipped us off, walking across for a better

view of the Sound, I didn't think about echoes,
only how long and narrow the tunnel,

and curved, and in the middle,
totally dark.

And winding my way to sunlight
distant as real life seen through a telescope turned around,

I could have been Jonah,
I could have been Giopetto,

for all the world forsaken in the steel-plated belly
of a whale, or fairy tale, taking

comfort in faith, in ends foreseeable   (this
tunnel built fifty years back to repel an invasion that never did happen:

inconceivable, halfway around the world
our soldiers today making Smart Bombs for Baghdad),

I almost believed in Salvation,
finding how long a single hum held in that ever-dark air:

how, like a chorus of angels, I
could project one tone, then two

then three, then four, adding
higher and higher in rapid harmony all

the notes of a single full chord
resounding together. Mystery suspended

where mystery was never intended to be.
In that tunnel, leading me on, my own voice.

"Gas. 1940"

After a painting by Edward Hopper

Perhaps you could call it nostalgia, this vision of three pumps
centered in concrete, shining red beacons lined up at attention and
taking up almost all of the bottom half of the frame,

where the attendant in long, clean, white shirtsleeves is even more centered,
and balding, and dwarfed against a backdrop of trees receding
into darkness or maybe emerging.

Sunrise. Sunset. Light hangs in suspension and shadows are such a gentle
gray; the sky barely blue; the road empty but not necessarily sad.

Maybe the feeling is promise, the way I once as a student, like all
good students, each day uncovered truths so profound
I felt the world's axis tilt, bravely claiming,

"All we can count on is change," as though no one had ever
said this before, and the same patterns would never recur. But then who
could have guessed Mobil's Pegasus high on this mast would ever surrender

to British Petroleum? That glamorous World War Two Rosie the Riveter
stories would last month show up in the news to prime us for war?

In this painting framed, like truth, in a time out of time—when everyone absent
is not yet overseas, part of that glamor, or home, skimping on rations—tv hasn't
been invented or brought more than one war into our living rooms, nightly
      all the new

ways we've found to kill each other and how much they cost, the cry
      "no blood for oil"
unthinkable, oil now needed to keep the pumps in this picture full forever
bleeding over a Gulf thousands of miles away.

This innocent road paved when Hiroshima still was only a word, and Stalin
a friend, only one of our many routes into denial.

Monika, before Reunification

Blue, blue eyes, and still she has wanted them bluer:
fluorescent blue lids above black
eyeliner, drawing

a zone between us that any other day I wouldn't have
bothered to cross, but here in Frankfurt I am
the guest, treated

after my lecture to green tortellini, red wine at noon
and my duty is still not over.
So Dresden, I ask,

indeed was depressing? expecting something surely
kin to guilt if not guilt itself:
how can we

the victorious walk those streets and not see firebombs?
Not remember who dropped them?
And Monika here

with her British accent (that until I lived a month in Britain
always sounded too prim to be true)
leaping past

all my carefully hidden assumptions, revealing
her own, what she hadn't
expected:

the greyness; how much destruction has not been rebuilt:
    a reminder:
We have deceived ourselves once.
Monika whom I can

no longer ignore, telling us *How much more honest than here*
in this colorful West, all of us thinking: We do
what we want to.

We buy. We spend. We set ourselves apart, choosing among
what is offered: visions we keep on
thinking are real.

In the Line of Vision

Something about the way the pool cue rests in the hand
and how the eye
all the way down the whole smooth length of it knows *this*

is it! even before
the chain reaction: light speed the connection:
pocket to ball to cue to your hand to your eye the center
        of everything, oh

this does not happen always and not always at will, and it's not
about winning, not
about power, it's something to do with whether or not you

are up to being true to that vision, your nerves
under control while keeping
your edge. Listen,

you bowlers out there, you know
the feeling the moment your fingers let go of that ball and it rolls
exactly as you hoped it would in that split-

second when every last one of your muscles suddenly leaned
into the line of your vision toward that one and
only spot the ball must strike for all

pins to fall. Have you
reader, never
had this experience? Your fingers on ivory, maybe,

gliding over the hardest *arpeggios*, following orders
not your own? That booth at the county fair, you feel it,
your dimes can't miss and by God

you bring home the fluffy stuffed elephant.
Just once in your life, at least, in touch with
some kind of harmony waiting for you to tune in?

And damned if I didn't surprise myself again in the pure
rush of it late last Sunday afternoon, with husband and nephew and Iowa
brother-in-law alongside the barbed-wire fencepost I said I wouldn't lean

the gun against—that was for beginners and weaklings—and though
this was my first time ever to pull a trigger of whatever
sort, I had my pride, I laid the barrel

against my cheek the way Dick said
I set my sights through both top notches
butt tight to my chest and as my index finger flexed I knew

as certain as I live and breathe it wouldn't be a bull's eye
but it would
hit the tree a hundred yards away and not

blitz a track through the soybeans beyond.
And damned if the sudden smoke thick in my nostrils didn't smell
        like reward.
If the thunderous report didn't bother my ears at all, although

earlier, standing two feet away and watching the others the pain
had me afraid. And damned if up until that day the woman
writing these lines had all her life hated the whole idea of guns as much

as she hated words spoken without experience, words not up
          to being true.
Truth was, that gun felt good in her hands,
and in that flash she saw how it might feel next time

to shoot at something moving. Maybe living. For the first time ever
this other kind of connection: something about the human condition:
too big to ignore, too close: the way

in Eugene in 1980 at breakfast we heard Mount St. Helens erupting
more than a hundred miles away. Friends in Portland, right at its door,
heard nothing. They said they heard nothing at all.

Words of Our Time

And have our tongues always not known what they speak?
    Good students, smart as whips, always
    hitting the books before killing the lights

Armed with knowledge, and struck by new ideas, who wasn't
    proud to take stabs at it,
    firing off questions like shots in the dark?

Dead right, dead wrong,
there was always a time we could talk without thinking of
    dressing to kill. Drowning our sorrows.

Parties were blasts, or they bombed.
No joke was ever caught dead without
    its punch line.

And here is a time when a president says
    we still have a shot at peace
    and the surest way to peace is through war

When the media says
    fire that kills you is friendly
    when it's from your own side

When we who say
    Bring our troops home
    are told we don't support them

In this time when words
can make any war just
    and peace, a smashing success

In this time, words
like feathers
    knock some of us over

And some of us stand
    speechless.

The History of Strife

When your teenage daughter sent my teenage daughter home
        in tears, and not
for the typical reasons—bad hair, fashion, boys—but for taking pride
in starting to master the German tongue my own

parents had, since childhood, abandoned (*Language of Evil, Jew-killer Language*),
the birthright to vengeance was on your daughter's side and she hurled it.

And I —who haven't thought of this in years, having chosen not to blame
you, the parents, blaming instead Our Cultural Climate, the Great
Human Condition—see you by chance and here it is

the stone of this memory rises as stones are not supposed to do
and I am struck, my own rage rises, this earthly hunger
to cast it back at you: fellow teachers, colleagues

whose allegiance to words, like mine, has always been steadfast
whose hope, like mine, is to change the history of strife
whose child I cannot forget hurt mine:

teachers to whom, if these hands had not a life
of their own, I would surrender
this poem.

Taps

This is what happens

Day is done   *(This is not)*

       Each time the flag gets folded
       each time a mother arranges her grief

Gone the sun   *(This is not)*

       Each time the camera focuses in
       on her face that will not crumble,
       the tears that will not come

From the hills   *(This is not)*
From the plain   *(This is not)*
From the sky   *(Not her son)*

       Not even when the guns go off

All is well   *(Not her son)*

       Not even when the flag is properly
       placed in her outstretched arms

    Safely rest   *(His skin, pollen on*
                                   butterfly wings)

    God is nigh   *(Sweet fontanel pulsing)*

       Hers to keep for ever and ever

Testament

If the hour had been a bit later, not so close
to supper
    ourselves, we'd eaten out, we had to, our friends' kitchen sink
        was plugged,
  we were guests, you know what I mean, what a mess

If she'd known we were coming, if we hadn't dropped in
without calling
        there wasn't a phone, but Chad was sure they wouldn't mind;
  they liked to talk; he'd been there before, he's a linguist, he knew

If she'd had an electric, not wood-burning stove;
or had dishes in sight; or mealtime smells
      she offered us freshly-made grape juice, she offered us brownies
  she didn't know what to make of our problems with plumbing

And had she not eight but just one or two children

If the boys still awake, at 8 p.m., hadn't been
wearing clothes clean like you wouldn't believe
      white shirts, suspenders, straight pins for buttons,
  straight chairs facing us all in a row

If all of her wooden floors shining in candlelight
hadn't been mopped after supper by two of those boys
      and this being Thursday not Saturday night, to hear her
  you'd think it the usual thing

If one of those boys, reciting for us his Bible verse, had
for even one moment faltered

oh, the bright moons of all of their faces hearing us speak, as though
nothing but goodness could shine from us

And had they been able to speak and read only English, not also
three kinds of German

Would I in that simple, friendly farmhouse deep inside Indiana still
have felt myself deep in some other country?
      The first thing I saw in her kitchen was all that radiant
space in the center, an apron open to gather us in

Would I find myself here, days later, still lame
for words for it, calling them home
        serenity, grace, dear
carrier pigeons of childhood lessons

Words (*certainty, peace*) that never will fit what I saw
in Diane's face as she ushered us into that kitchen
        a church we haven't been to in years, *no matter,*
nothing can matter more than this moment

Words for what I heard in her voice, an arm
one gives to the blind
        here is the step, now,
here we turn

This lullaby, untranslatable

        Sweet, sweet, the trust in her eyes
        Sweet light from her candles, a shield
        Inside her voice, no one can stumble
        Outside of this house the whole world

Good Friday: Wendell, Idaho

Everywhere here the sound of water,
Not just the river the other side of the fish ponds,
Rumbling far away and deep between these far canyon walls

Not just the fish ponds, spilling
Rim over rim a thin continuous curtain, ninety-
Six steps at a time, you can count them, and not

Just the flashing cascades springing out of the rock
Wall behind the house, frantic
In their release from miles of underground highways

But the whole of it all, an absolution
The friends who live here have learned to
Live with, where is the pain of the world?

Good Fridays of childhood always we'd go to church,
The services ending precisely at 3: 00, the time
Christ is said to have died, and I took the sorrow

Into myself, it happened again, and always,
It seemed, it rained, which was fitting, and always
We left the church heads down.

Here, over the river, over my perch on the housefront
Steps, a goose
Flaps past the first star.

Crows, hawks, circle.
Ducks bank into clouds. A heron,
Feet trailing the question mark crook of its neck,

Rises out of a pond. Here,
Far from home and all need to go on, waiting for
My friends to return, I could believe

The smell of sage on my fingers will last forever.
The cry of the male pheasant rising from grass, his hen
Clucking a trail below, will ring forever, with water

Deep in my ears. And I will always see the porcupine maybe
Five feet away, maybe less, that I almost didn't
See on my walk, the perfect camouflage nibbling low-growing sage,

A sunburst of quills like grasses, the back
Side of a war bonnet, perfectly still, head cocked to one side,
That one shining black eye turned to mine.

Mukilteo Ferry

After the long drive north, relentless
the traffic, relentless the heightened news of yet
another alert

after each car, each truck, has clanged
from dock to steel-plated deck and parked, and I get out
to stand at the stern—

light wind, clouds breaking,
and the quaking of tethered engines,
beyond this iron chain the dark water churning—

without warning, the cloak of a great
calm descends upon me, like
the very word

"upon"—the way
it slows the sentence down—
a measured word, hinged—the way

fish, in their inscrutable
expressions, hang
immobile, as though rooted

each to its own place—
and I enter again into the beneficence
of the world of water

whose rhythms will not be hurried
into whose covenant,
under the ancient composure of stars,

we pull anchor and begin to sail.

Notes

"Offerings" was written for Dorothy and William Stafford.

"The Thing to Do" takes place at the D.H. Lawrence Ranch, Taos, New Mexico.

"Blessed Among Birds" is dedicated to my husband, Ralph Salisbury. Benson Pond is on the Malheur National Wildlife Refuge, 60 miles south of Burns, Oregon.

"Columbus and Me" is dedicated to Professors Stephen Dow Beckham and Dell Hymes, whose lifelong devotion to the history, language, and literature of the Native peoples of Oregon, has enriched my own research and understanding.

"Epithalamion from Norway" is for Kim Stafford and Perrin Kerns.

"Finnmark, an Idyl." Finnmark, technically the northernmost county of Norway, is a name used conversationally for Sápmi—the land of the Sámi (Laplander) people—which stretches, above the Arctic Circle, over four countries: Norway, Sweden, Finland and Russia. The poet referred to in this poem is the late Nils-Aslak Valkeapää. His home was in the far north of Finland, just a few miles over the border with Norway. For further exploration of Finnmark/Sápmi, and the Sámi people, please go to the following site http://www.visitnorthcape.com/home.html and click on history and culture.

"This Side of Paradise." The setting is Frederiksted, St. Croix.

"Museums." Multnomah Falls is west of Portland, Oregon, above the Columbia River.

"Questions of Grace" and other poems set in Norway were begun in Tromsø, Norway, where my husband, Ralph Salisbury, was working on translations of work by Sámi (Laplander) poet Nils-Aslak Valkeapää. My thanks to the Norwegian Fulbright Commission, the University of Tromsø, to Nils-Aslak Valkeapää, and to the Gaski-Rajala family, for their support and warm welcome.

"Lines Begun While Hearing Charles Wright Read" is printed with the knowledge and backing of Charles Wright.

"Report from Tromsø." Approximately 250 miles north of the Arctic Circle, Tromsø, Norway, is an island city of 50,000.

The landscape described in "Still Life" is near Hammingberg, Norway. This poem is dedicated to Britt Rajala.

"Even the Stones Have Names" takes place on the Gaski family ancestral land in Vestre Seida, Norway, on the Tana River. It is dedicated to Harald Gaski and to his mother, Kristine Gaski. The Sámi (Laplander) name for Seida is Sieiddá, meaning small sacrificial stone.

"First Morning in the Santa Caterina: Villa Serbelloni, Bellagio" is one of several poems in this book written while in residence for five weeks at the Rockefeller Study and Conference Center, Bellagio, Italy. I am indebted also to Naomi Shihab Nye, whose poem, "The Comfort of Wood" (from *Different Ways to Pray*), begins with the line: "I come to this table tired."

"Surgeonfish" takes place, in part, at Ras Mohammed National Park, Egypt. The television program is the Lehrer News Hour, November 6, 1995, following the assassination of Israeli prime minister Ytzhak Rabin. I dedicate this poem to Glen Thompson, young writer of conscience, whose sense of social responsibility and justice continues to be an inspiration to me.

"Words of Our Time," dedicated to Chilean poet Jorge Montealegre, is in response to his poem titled *"Palabras del Tiempo."* The president referred to is George Bush.

"The History of Strife." My thanks to Paulann Petersen for this title, which comes from lines in her poem "Resolution," from *The Wild Awake*.

"Testament" is for Helen Frost and Chad Thompson, and for their Amish friends Dan and Diane Schmucker, in Indiana.

"Porcupine at Dusk" and "Good Friday: Wendell, Idaho" are for Kathleen, Regen, and Sarah Armstrong, managing a trout farm along the Snake River.

Ingrid Wendt, born and raised in the American midwest, has taught and traveled extensively throughout the Western American states and in Europe. She has won the Yellowglen Award with *The Angle of Sharpest Ascending* (poetry); the Oregon Book Award in Poetry with *Singing the Mozart Requiem*; the Carolyn Kizer award from *Calapooya Collage;* and the D.H. Lawrence Award. Her other books include *Blow the Candle Out* (poetry); *Moving the House* (poetry); *From Here We Speak: An Anthology of Oregon Poetry; In Her Own Image: Women Working in the Arts;* and *Starting With Little Things: A Guide to Writing Poetry in the Classroom.* Her 30 years with state- and privately-funded arts programs have taken her into hundreds of classrooms where she has introduced poetry writing to many thousands of students, grades K-12. She has taught also at the college and university levels, including the MFA Program of Antioch University Los Angeles, and in Germany as a three-time Senior Fulbright Professor. A frequent presenter at teacher workshops and conferences, and a popular keynote speaker, she lives in Eugene, Oregon, with her husband, poet and writer Ralph Salisbury. Visit her author website at www.ingridwendt.com.